A Giant Egg

and

Fluffy Feathers

Ruby Tuesday Books

Whose Little Baby Are You?

by Ellen Lawrence

Published in 2016 by Ruby Tuesday Books Ltd.

Editor: Mark J. Sachner
Designer: Emma Randall
Production: John Lingham

Photo Credits:
Cosmographics: 23 (top); FLPA: 8–9, 10 (top), 11, 12, 19;
Getty Images: 13; Shutterstock: Cover, 1, 4–5, 6–7, 10
(bottom), 14–15, 16–17, 18, 20–21, 22, 23.

Library of Congress Control Number: 2015940229

ISBN 978-1-910549-20-9

Printed and published in the United States of America

For further information including rights and
permissions requests, please contact our Customer
Service Department at 877-337-8577.

Contents

Words shown in **bold** in the text are
explained in the glossary.

A Grassland Chick

On a hot, dusty **grassland**, there lives a little chick.

Grassland

The baby bird is just a few days old.

He has a long, speckled neck, and his body is covered with feathers.

Chick

Feathers

Who does this little baby belong to?

The little chick belongs to a mother and father ostrich.

Ostriches are the biggest birds in the world.

They are much taller than an adult human!

Father ostrich

The father ostrich has black and white feathers.

The mother ostrich has brown feathers.

Using his huge feet, the father ostrich scratched a **shallow** nest hole in the dusty soil.

Then the mother ostrich laid seven eggs in the nest.

Other females came to the nest and laid their eggs, too.

These females don't help take care of their eggs, though.

An ostrich
waiting to lay
her eggs

Mother ostrich

Eggs

Soon, the mother and father ostrich had 21 eggs to care for!

Ostrich eggs

They took turns sitting on the eggs.

Mother ostrich sitting on eggs

The parent birds protected the eggs from baboons, hyenas, and other egg-eating **predators**.

Father ostrich sitting on eggs

Now, 42 days have passed since the eggs were laid.

Suddenly—peck, peck, peck!

A little chick is **hatching** from his egg.

Ostrich chick

Beak

Eggshell

He pecks hard at the eggshell with his beak and pushes with his little feet.

Foot

The baby ostrich is a little wobbly, but he's soon walking around.

Within hours, more chicks have hatched.

Ostrich chick

Father ostrich

Ostrich chicks

The mother and father ostrich keep watch for lions, cheetahs, and other predators.

If a predator comes close, the brave father bird chases it away.

Mother ostrich

Ostriches eat grass, leaves, roots, flowers, and seeds.

The little ostrich watches his parents peck at food.

He copies his mom and dad, and is soon pecking at plants.

A one-week-old ostrich chick

The ostrich chick spends his days looking for food with his family.

A three-month-old ostrich chick

The young ostriches grow bigger and taller.

A six-month-old ostrich

Now, if a predator comes close, they run away.

Ostriches can run at 40 miles an hour (64 km/h).

An adult male ostrich

By the time he is one year old, the young ostrich is ready to take care of himself.

At four years old, he has become an adult with black and white feathers.

An adult female ostrich

Now the ostrich finds a **mate**.

Together, the pair of ostriches will raise chicks of their own.

Fact File

All About Ostriches

Ostrich foot

An ostrich's eye measures 2 inches (5 cm) across.

An ostrich has just two large toes on each foot. Most birds have three or four toes on each foot.

Ostriches have wings, but they are too heavy to fly.

Adult ostriches usually live in small groups.

An adult ostrich can kill a lion with a single kick.

Ostrich Size

Woman

Man

Adult ostrich

Ostrich Weight

Adult ostrich:
200 to 350 pounds (91-159 kg)

Newly hatched chick:
2 pounds (0.9 kg)

22

Where Do Ostriches Live?

N
W E
S

Asia

Europe

North
America

Atlantic
Ocean

Africa

Indian
Ocean

Pacific
Ocean

South
America

Australia

Ostriches live wild in Africa. They live on grasslands and in dry deserts in the areas shown in red.

Eggs and Chicks

An ostrich egg can weigh more than 3 pounds (1.36 kg).

A newly hatched baby ostrich is about the size of an adult chicken. It grows about 12 inches (30.5 cm) taller each month.

An ostrich egg

A mother ostrich sits on her eggs in the daytime. She blends in with the brown land, making it hard for predators to see her.

A father ostrich sits on the eggs at night. His black feathers make it hard for predators to see him in the darkness.

23

Glossary

grassland (GRASS-land)
A habitat covered with grasses and other low-growing plants. Only a few trees grow on a grassland.

hatching (HACH-ing)
Breaking out of an egg.

mate (MATE)
An animal's partner with which it has babies.

predator (PRED-uh-tur)
An animal that hunts and eats other animals.

shallow (SHAL-oh)
Not very deep.

Index

Read More

Gibbs, Maddie. *Ostriches (Safari Animals)*. New York: Rosen Publishing (2011).

Lunis, Natalie. *Ostrich: The World's Biggest Bird (Super Sized!)*. New York: Bearport Publishing (2007).

Learn More Online

To learn more about ostriches, go to
www.rubytuesdaybooks.com/whoselittlebaby